11/07

CAREER BUILDING THROUGH
DIGITAL PHOTOGRAPHY

RICK DOBLE

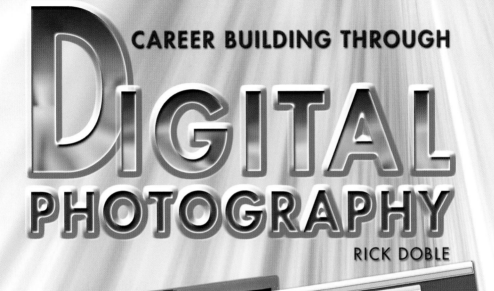

ROSEN
PUBLISHING®
New York

To my wife, Janet, who has been my best friend for thirty years

Published in 2008 by The Rosen Publishing Group, Inc.
29 East 21st Street, New York, NY 10010

Library of Congress Cataloging-in-Publication Data

Doble, Rick
Career building through digital photography / Rick Doble. — 1st ed.
   p. cm. — (Digital career building)
Includes bibliographical references and index.
ISBN-13: 978-1-4042-1941-0
ISBN-10: 1-4042-1941-2
1. Photography—Vocational guidance. 2. Photography—Digital techniques. I. Title.
TR154.D63 2007
775023—dc22

                                                    2006102732

Manufactured in the United States of America

CONTENTS

CHAPTER ONE

THE DIGITAL REVOLUTION

Digital photography is everywhere. No matter where you go, it seems like everyone is taking pictures. With people using everything from low-resolution cell phone cameras to professional single-lens reflex (SLR) cameras to capture images, digital photography has taken over.

In just a few years, the digital format has surpassed traditional film cameras to become the most important development in the medium. About 80 percent of today's professional photographers shoot with digital cameras. In fact, digital cameras have outsold film cameras since 2002. Young people are leading the way in digital photography, too, since about two-thirds of digital camera owners are less than thirty years of age.

The majority of digital camera owners are young people. One of the huge pluses of digital photography is that it allows you to view your shot immediately.

Like the revolution in information-sharing that occurred with the use of personal computers and the Internet, the digital photography format is breaking new ground. Shooting with a digital camera has many advantages, including the ability to evaluate your images instantly to ensure that you have achieved the best possible shot. In addition, experimenting with different methods of shooting is made much more economical with the digital format because you do not have the added expense of film or film developing.

Changing the Rules

Most photographers agree that the greatest advantage of digital is the ability to see their photographs quickly. Because your images can be seen immediately, you can shoot something or someone repeatedly if you need to make corrections or adjustments. Because pictures can be modified with computer software, photographers have increased control over their final images with the ability to adjust contrast and color. In addition, digital photography is much less expensive than film photography, digital cameras tend to be lighter, and photos can be shared easily over the Internet with friends or family. Images can also be sent electronically in seconds to editors of publications anywhere in the world.

This revolution in photography did not happen overnight. The first digital sensor that could record a light image was invented in 1969. In the 1980s, Sony introduced the Mavica (which used a floppy disc), but it was not a true digital camera. It was not until the mid-1990s that personal digital cameras became more readily

Digital photography gives the photographer the power to view, modify, send, and share pictures more easily than ever before.

available. Sales were strong, and within eight years, more digital cameras were being sold than regular film cameras.

Today there are hundreds of digital cameras, from point-and-shoot devices costing less than $100, to SLR cameras that cost more than $1,000. Many cell phones are also equipped with small camera devices, so just about everyone has a digital camera at his or her disposal.

A CLOSER LOOK You can familiarize yourself with most professional-grade digital equipment and software by visiting www.slrtoday.com, where you can find product reviews, technical information, and photography tips and tutorials.

Because photos can be sent electronically or placed immediately on the Internet, sharing digital images and networking with people is simple. Digital photos can be added to photo-sharing sites like Flickr (www.flickr.com), Shutterfly (www.shutterfly.com), Photobucket (photobucket.com), and Picasa (picasa.google.com). Or they can be posted on more individual Web sites where you have complete control over the look, feel, and navigation of your work. (Chapter three will describe these methods in detail.) Because your images are already in a digital format, they can be sent as files attached to an e-mail message or displayed in the design of a newsletter, Web site, brochure, or press release.

Shoot for Fun, Shoot for Profit

Whatever method of displaying pictures is used, digital photography and the Internet offer photographers much greater exposure than was possible years ago. Instead of appealing to a local audience, a photographer can now reach out globally to an entire network of like-minded people who appreciate his or her work. Before the Internet, a creative person was limited to finding an audience within his or her community; however, photographers can now be in touch with people anywhere there is a computer. For instance, a photographer keeping a journal of images, or a blog, can find a niche that would have been unthinkable years ago.

While anyone can take snapshots, the makings of a good photograph are in its originality or what it reveals about a specific moment in time. A great

photographer develops an intense curiosity about his or her subject, and pursues it over time to fully express him- or herself.

The business of photography has also been transformed. With freelance photographers making up about half of the people employed in photography, freelancers now can work with editors, publications, Web sites, and special-interest groups anywhere in the world. For the ambitious and hardworking, it means that new job opportunities are always available for those willing to ferret them out. It also means that there are many new outlets for their work. Virtually every Web site needs photography in some form. For example, the millions of Web sites, blogs, newsletters, and magazines that cover current events, today's fashions, or pop-culture trends require a constant supply of images. Some diligent photographers even carve out small markets for themselves, including specializing in unusual areas such as macro photography or by taking photos of snowflakes, butterflies, or beetles.

For a young person thinking about a career in photography, this is good news, but it also means that competition is fierce, especially because buying professional digital equipment is affordable and connecting with people is much faster.

Increasing Opportunities

While the business of digital photography has grown, the competition for jobs has increased too. Photographers who do succeed stand out in a number of ways: their work is of exceptional quality and is

Author Rick Doble's Web site (rickdoble.net) was launched from a remote, rural area in North Carolina. Nevertheless, his work reaches tens of thousands of people around the world every month.

professional, accurate, and delivered on time and as promised.

In addition, it would be a mistake to discuss the business of digital photography by itself. Over the past twenty years, a number of things have changed that have added to its growth. These developments include the widespread use of the Internet, professional desktop publishing software, and access to inexpensive long-distance communications, electronic payments, and fast nationwide package delivery.

For example, these new capabilities mean that even a digital photographer who is working in an isolated, rural area can reach a wide audience by displaying his or

her work on the Internet. A photographer can work for an editor that he or she never meets, but only talks to over the phone. Payments for images can be made to photographers very quickly and reliably via financial services such as PayPal or by direct bank deposit.

Even highly experimental photographers have been able to earn money by displaying their images on personal Web sites. Income can be generated through paid subscriptions, through the sale of work, through advertising, or by attracting opportunities from editors and print publications. If you are creative, innovative, and ambitious, opportunities are available right now that will help lead you on a path to a successful career in image making.

CHAPTER TWO

CITIZEN JOURNALISM

Digital photography has had a huge impact on the industry, especially in key markets. Photojournalism or documentary-style, "on the street" photography has been completely transformed because photographers can now view their photos right away. This immediacy ensures that they have captured their images as they wished. They then can rush those photographs to various major news agencies such as Reuters (www.reuters.com) and the Associated Press (www.ap.org), organizations that can enhance, resize, and distribute the pictures as needed. In a matter of hours after an event, the photos can be seen on the Internet or published in the latest edition of a newspaper or magazine.

This is the site for Reuters, an international news agency. Digital photographers send such sites images for instant posting on breaking stories.

DIGITAL PHOTOGRAPHY

There are a large number of Web sites and news organizations with a growing need for images. This constant demand provides an ever-increasing market for digital photographers. By utilizing the Internet, smaller news organizations such as Tribune Newspaper Network (www.newschoice.com) and McClatchy Newspapers (www.mcclatchy.com, which includes former Knight Ridder publications) can compete successfully with major news organizations, too. News Web sites targeted to niche audiences can stay up-to-date with a vast network of freelance photographers who are available to take pictures as needed.

More and more, large and small organizations are embracing what is now called citizen journalism, taking advantage of the fact that nearly everyone is equipped with some sort of camera. For instance, in 2005, when a string of bombings terrorized London, England, it was an amateur's image that captured the event. The photograph, of passengers rushing out of a smoky train, became the leading image that was seen the world over. With the success of Web sites like YouTube (www. youtube.com) and Flickr, citizen journalism is increasingly gaining respect.

Reuters, CNN, and Yahoo! request images from amateur photographers to illustrate their Web sites. CNN's "Exchange" (www.cnn.com/exchange) encourages readers to send images of specific events, while Reuters is developing a service devoted entirely to user-submitted photos. Photographers can also upload their images to a section of Yahoo! called "You Witness News"

(news.yahoo. com/page/youwitnessnews). Other Web sites offer amateurs the chance to get their images published in newspapers around the country and the world, including Scoopt (www.scoopt.com) and NowPublic (www.nowpublic.com).

Many Outlets

Desktop publishing often requires that photography be mixed with graphics for posters or pamphlets. Digital photography makes this task simple because the photograph and graphic elements, such as type or boxes, can be easily blended. This need naturally extends to the Internet.

Other areas of the field have gone through major changes due to the impact of digital photography. Fashion photographers like digital formats because they can easily correct or rework the image. For example, in digital fashion shots, models' eyes are usually brightened, their teeth are whitened, and any blemishes or scars on the skin are retouched.

Digital photography has virtually revolutionized business, too. In the fast-moving real estate market, digital allows comprehensive pictures of a home to be put online quickly so that a house can sell in a matter of weeks instead of months. Auction houses now offer prospective bidders digital images of items available for purchase, and fashion houses can send digital pictures of designers' samples to retailers in seconds. The uses of digital photography and the advantages it provides are seemingly endless.

With all of those advantages, you might think that traditional film would no longer be used. Nevertheless,

Digital photography is needed in every part of the country for the real estate business. Quality pictures help sell a property quickly, as on this Web site (century21.com).

some photographers still prefer regular film when it comes to high-quality portrait work. In these cases, professional photographers often use large-format cameras that house a larger negative than typical 35mm. (The larger the negative, the better the quality of print.) Film has a high resolution and soft painterly quality that cannot be matched by digital. This is especially true if the client wants super-sized enlargements of a family portrait, for example. Furthermore, in the well-paying portraiture business, the additional expense of film is not important. In this case, digital has had less of an impact.

Going High-Tech

Because digital photography is so simple and inexpensive, many photographers now take hundreds of photos of their subject instead of dozens. While this gives the photographer a greater selection to choose from, it means that he or she must spend hours editing, cataloging, and storing his or her images. He or she must also create a systemized retrieval system, so that months or years later, specific images can be easily found. Since large, high-resolution digital images require a huge amount of storage space, most photographers will create a backup copy of their work on a second (in most cases, external) hard drive. This means that photographers have to manage not just the primary cataloging and retrieval system, but also the backup system. Another backup method would be to burn your images to disc and use a physical cataloging system. Many photographers prefer to do both.

Although it may be faster, digital photography makes additional technology demands on the user. A photographer must be completely comfortable with computers and the terminology involved. He or she must have a thorough understanding of professional photo-enhancing and manipulating software such as Adobe PhotoShop and Apple's Aperture. These programs can be complicated to learn and may take some time with which to become familiar. (You can also ask your retailer for a stripped-down version of Adobe PhotoShop for beginners that is easier to use and less expensive to buy. Many digital cameras come with

Sophisticated software programs make it easy to fine-tune or radically change a photograph after it is shot.

some image-enhancing software geared toward typical computer users.)

A PhotoShop tutorial for beginners can be found at: http://epaperpress.com/psphoto. PaintShop Pro is a less expensive program that many people like. You can find it at http://www.jasc.com.

Despite its obvious speed and ease of use, digital does have its disadvantages. For instance, if a digital camera breaks during a shoot, the photographer cannot fix it, whereas the older mechanical cameras could often be repaired in a timely fashion.

The Old Rules Still Apply

There is a saying that the more things change, the more they remain the same. This is certainly true of photography. Although many of the tools and methods have changed, the skills and qualities that make a first-class photographer remain the same.

Photography has been, and still is, a deadline business. Photographers deal with deadlines constantly, from arriving to an event on time, to scheduling a shooting session with individuals during the event, to delivering the images by the deadline. Reliability is a key quality. In fact, a very good photographer who delivers work as promised will often fair better than a more gifted photographer who has trouble meeting deadlines.

A photograph is only as good as the photographer behind the lens, who has experience and understands lighting, composition, and all the elements that make an eye-catching image. For example, effective lighting is critical for every image. Photographers who have spent many hours studying and working with lighting will create much better pictures than those who have not, especially because they can readily anticipate their needs in any given situation.

For any photographer, a sense of timing is critical. Photographers must often work in changing or dangerous situations. Photojournalists are required to be in the right place at the right time. It can take many years to learn how to master this sense of timing and anticipation.

All photographers need to be able to manage and maintain their equipment. This includes cameras and

lenses, flashes, storage devices, tripods, and lights. All equipment must be in top condition, and the photographer must have a thorough understanding of how his or her hardware works. Good photographers spend a significant amount of time checking their equipment and making sure that they arrive at a job with backups whenever possible, such as additional memory cards, battery power, lights, and bulbs. Bringing a small notebook and pencil or pen is also useful to jot down correct name spellings or to note locations or information about exposures.

Freelance vs. Staff Positions

Many jobs require that a photographer be able to work harmoniously with a lot of different people. Unless a photographer is shooting scientific subjects or products, he or she works with various individuals at news events, weddings and parties, sports arenas, or political rallies. An ability to work smoothly with people is essential to getting the best shots.

Photographers today generally operate in one of two ways: either they are hired in salaried positions, or they take freelance jobs. Salaried positions usually require a college degree. People without a degree, but with talent and drive, can establish their own freelance business. While freelance photography does not require a degree, it still requires that the photographer have considerable experience.

About half of digital photographers work on a freelance basis. They have access to many more outlets than ever before. Those people who have a variety of digital skills in addition to photography, such as desktop

Digital Photographer Martin Fuchs

Martin Fuchs is a young and successful freelance photographer with a detailed personal photoblog (www.journalofaphotographer.com) that explains and displays his work and how he came to succeed. He first worked as a graphics designer, but then decided to take the plunge into photography because that was his true love. In the beginning, he landed an internship with Mangum Photos in New York City. This job got him started and allowed him to make important contacts. For his internship, he created a six-month photoblog of New York (www.newyorkphotoblog.com) that he updated every day. He now freelances around the world for major magazines and newspapers, and has a number of corporate clients. In addition, he was able to get corporate sponsorship to pay for his software and equipment. He lists these sponsors on his personal blog. By being ambitious, professional, approachable, and reliable, Fuchs has become very accomplished. You can review his portfolio at www.martinfuchs.com.

publishing, computer graphics, journalism, or Web design, can do very well.

Salaried jobs in photography often require at least an associate degree. These jobs include scientific and medical photography for those who work at hospitals or who assist medical professionals in their research. Government salaried jobs in photography can include police surveillance, forensics, and travel photography. Industrial photographers do diverse jobs for a company; they might

This model is wearing an expensive parka. An exciting photograph of her in this outfit may help sell the clothing.

take product shots, portraits of managers and workers, document employee events, or shoot landscapes for the annual report. Stores and malls need photographers for their products, catalogs, and events. Larger establishments may hire full-time, salaried photographers. Advertising also provides high-paying positions for artistic photographers.

The military needs photographers in all branches for a variety of needs. Students who do not want to attend college could be employed or learn the trade in the U.S. Army, Air Force, Navy, Marines, Coast Guard, National Guard, or Reserves. This is exactly the route of some of history's most famous photographers.

CHAPTER THREE

EVALUATING
YOUR GOALS

If you have been taking digital pictures for some time, and friends and family admire your work, then you are already on your way to developing digital photography into a skill. This can be of help to you no matter what field of study you choose, or you can turn your interest and love of photography into a career by itself.

By now you probably have a clear idea about which subjects you want to photograph. These subject areas could lead to a career or could work together with other goals. For instance, if you enjoy shooting school sporting events such as football, basketball, or baseball games, or even people practicing alternative sports like skateboarding or motocross, this interest

To develop a career in digital photography, shoot people, places, and events that interest you. Try to learn as much about photography as you can.

could lead to work for television stations, newspapers, or magazines.

If you instead prefer to take portraits of your friends and fellow students, then a future in portrait and wedding photography might be something to consider. Yet another recent trend in photography has been to shoot pet portraits.

 Jim Dratfield, a photographer who has been profiled on television's *20/20* and CNN, has made an entire career out of photographing America's four-legged pals. In addition, he has published eight books, has been featured in countless magazines, and has a list of clients that include Visa and AT&T. His work can be seen at www.petography.com.

If you like to take pictures of events at your school and document important issues that are being debated, your interests could evolve into a career in photojournalism.

Or you might like to take pictures of fashion shows at the local mall or specialize in shots of local rock bands. These interests could lead to a career in the fashion industry.

Or maybe you just prefer to take pictures on vacation; years from now, you could be employed as a travel photographer. Other specialized fields are industrial and product photography. If you tend to focus on photos of science projects or butterflies, then these specialties might be for you.

Even students who are hoping to work as filmmakers or film directors can benefit from learning about photography. Still photography is a great way to get started in

Author Rick Doble shot this photo through a rain-covered windshield as his car was moving. Unusual photographs such as this one have been sold for book and CD covers.

moving film. Many famous directors such as Stanley Kubrick and Larry Clark began as still photographers and then evolved into filmmakers. Still photography is especially useful because it teaches composition, a skill that is essential to filmmaking, but one that is less obvious when the camera or subject is moving.

Other Uses of Photography

Because photography is so versatile, it is a good skill to learn no matter which career you choose. Just about every subject is better explained and illustrated with a photograph or two. If you are thinking about going into urban planning, for example, knowing how to take photos

of neighborhoods is very useful. Anthropologists and archaeologists need photos of dig sites. Writers need images to accompany their stories. If you are thinking about working in a medical field, photos of procedures or documenting injuries or ailments could be important. Even people working in the insurance business are in constant need of quality photos. Knowing how to take pictures for business, marketing, medicine, political science, or sociology might give you an edge if you choose to study one of these fields.

There is virtually no limit to the areas of study that you might find interesting. Most subjects can be developed and expanded so that you can apply them later in life to just about any interest or career path. What really matters is the quality of your work. As long as you take clear, well-composed, and eye-catching photos, your work should find an outlet.

Starting Out

If you already have a number of top-notch photographs that have appeared in your school newspaper or on flyers for a local rock band, then you have a great start. The next step is to organize your work into a format that you can easily share with others so that you can build a network of people who look at your work critically and who may offer you jobs.

Since roughly 90 percent of teens use the Internet, and nearly 60 percent of blogs are being created by teens, the Internet is the obvious place to begin displaying your photographs as you build your skills and portfolio. This is an excellent way to get started because you can do it at your own pace with no deadlines. You can contribute as much or as little as you like, it is often free, and it will force you to constantly update and reevaluate your work. Placing your photos on the Web will also help you create a network of people who respond to your work. There are three basic types of Web sites where photography can be displayed.

Picture-Sharing Web Sites

Picture-sharing Web sites are easy to create and often free. These sites are perfect for people who are good at photography but not fully familiar with posting and updating work on the Internet. While you can pick from a variety of layouts, you will usually be confined to working within a pre-set design. These often look like photo albums with many small images. Clicking on each image displays the full-size photo. Viewers can often post comments or vote for their favorite picture. Some sites even allow users to send new images directly from cell phones.

 Once you have your photos on the Internet, you can use the beta tags on some photo-sharing Web sites to gain exposure to your work. Web sites like Flickr use beta tags, and in so doing, allow people to search for specific images. Some of these people are often editors and art directors looking for photos to illustrate print and Web publications. If you register your work under a creative commons (CC) license (meaning that others can freely use your images when they give you credit), your photos may turn up in surprising places.

If you would prefer to limit who can see your work, picture sharing is a good way to go. You can send e-mails to particular people on a regular basis, and they can view your work without having to be a member of the picture-sharing Web site. As mentioned before, some picture-sharing sites are Photobucket.com, Flickr.com, and Yahoo! Photos. Some of these sites allow you to host and link your images to social networks like MySpace.com and to blogs and message boards. With the Internet changing so fast, other picture-sharing sites are likely to emerge. For the latest listings of such sites, search Google for "picture sharing" or "photo sharing."

 While social networks such as MySpace might seem like a good place to display photos, they are of lesser value for serious photographers, since most place a limit on the overall size and number of images that can be uploaded. A better solution is to join a photo-sharing group and link your photo display to your profile. If you decide to create a blog or Web site, you can link pictures from photo-sharing sites.

Photoblogs

Photoblogs are more sophisticated than picture-sharing Web sites, and like photo-sharing Web sites, they are usually available for use free of charge. A blog is like a personal Web site that's meant to represent a slice of your life or experience—sort of like a journal or a personal diary. Instead of your photos collecting in a repository, images in a photoblog are meant to work together in a more meaningful, related way. If you feel comfortable

The Eyefetch.com site allows you to chose, customize, and design your own photoblog. Look at various blogs on this site to discover the possibilities that exist for you.

uploading your images to the Internet and doing simple HTML (hypertext markup language) modifications, then a blog could be for you. Blogs are fun because they may offer the creator more feedback from viewers in a comments section.

While photoblogs can be limited to only those you notify, they can also be public. Most photoblog sites, such as Eyefetch.com, Blockstar.com, Photobloggers.net, and Photoblog.be, have user-friendly interfaces allowing you to choose from a variety of pre-made templates, but you can also modify your template or create your own. They are easy to use, and you should browse a number of them before deciding on which one best appeals to you.

DIGITAL PHOTOGRAPHY

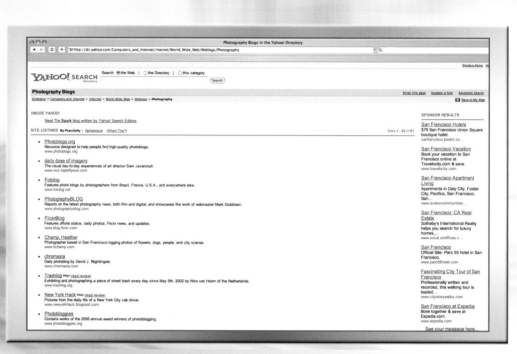

The Yahoo! directory (http://dir.yahoo.com) lists the latest quality individual photoblogs, as well as sites that search and locate photoblogs.

Before choosing which photoblog site is right for you, visit the following directories: www.photoblogs.org, DMOZ Directory of Photoblogs (dmoz.org/Arts/Photography/Weblogs/Photoblogs), and Yahoo! Photoblogs (dir.yahoo.com/Computers_and_ Internet/Internet/World_Wide_Web/Weblogs/Photography).

Photoblogs are a flexible and good way to get started with displaying your photographs online. If you later decide to have your own Web site, you can change the location of your blog and "publish" it as part of your Web site. In this way your blog can continue to be part of your online work, even when you have upgraded to an individual Web site.

If a number of people at your school want to create a blog together, then a group blog is an ideal option. According to Blogger.com, "Group blogs can be excellent communication tools for small teams, families, or other groups. Give your group its own space on the Web for sharing news, links, and ideas."

Personal Web Sites

For maximum control and exposure, personal Web sites cannot be beat. Although they are not free, they can cost as little as $100 a year. With your own Web site, you can control the look, feel, exhibits, linking, and navigation, as well as the background material about you and your work.

For example, if you already have many photos, you can organize these into separate galleries that will work together much better than a photoblog. Generally speaking, a Web site will get more traffic than a blog or a picture-sharing site will, so in creating one, you can reach a much larger audience. You can invite comments, set up a guestbook, and encourage people to send you e-mail. With free software, you can also track which and how many pages of your site are being viewed, plus how people are finding your Web site and for what reasons. With this information you can build a network of people who like your work and who may offer you jobs. Having your own Web site, as opposed to a photoblog, sends a signal that you are very committed to your work.

Background material about you and your photography is equally important. If you are looking for photography jobs, for example, you should have an updated

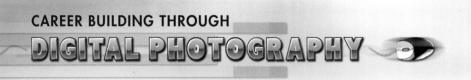
résumé on your Web page, which shows that you are professional, reliable, and serious about your work.

If you have published a photoblog for a while, then a Web site might be a good next step. This requires that you understand FTP, HTML, and how to create Web pages that can be indexed and successfully located by search engines.

No matter which method of display you choose, each will have a unique Web address for your work. Use this address when e-mailing people or on business cards. In addition, always double-check that you did what you thought you did on the Internet. For example, after uploading pictures to a picture-sharing site or blog, look at your site anew (which might require hitting the refresh button on your browser). Make sure that your new work is being displayed properly and as you desired.

Adding a counter to every page of your site allows you to track which pages are being viewed and the search words that are finding your pages. Many people don't think this step is necessary, but you may be surprised to discover why people are interested in your Web site. With sophisticated counters available for free, it is a mistake not to take advantage of them.

TECH TOOLS You can find free resources for creating Web sites at www.bravenet. com, www.gostats.com, and www.webtools4free.com.

While most of the feedback about your work will be positive, you will undoubtedly receive a few uncomplimentary e-mails, or "flames." This is to be expected. You cannot please everyone with your work,

Bravenet.com offers free tools for Web masters, plus Web design advice and lots of useful tips.

nor should you try. Unfortunately, this is part of putting your work online. You must take the negative criticism along with the positive feedback.

After your photos are online, you should explore local outlets for your work. Do not attempt to get jobs until you feel comfortable with the quality of your photographs and until you are certain that you can meet deadlines. If you take on a job before you are ready and miss a deadline, for example, you may find that other potential employers will avoid you.

Shooting for Experience

When starting out, you might have to work for free. This will give you valuable experience. Although the job may

MySpace (myspace.com) is a popular online community for young people. You can show your photos here directly or link images from an album site.

not offer financial compensation, you can list it on your résumé. Sometimes, shooting for free will allow you the opportunity to see a show or performance without cost to you. In other cases, you might be able to sell your pictures later if you pull off some great shots. For example, if you took extra pictures at a wedding and the bride decides she wants additional prints, you could sell them at a profit. In another example, you could take shots of a local rock band for free; later you might charge them for a desktop publishing layout for a poster or a CD cover using those images.

If you look for jobs that fulfill the demands of print media, understand that an image that looks good

How Photos Are Located by Search Engines

If you want your work to be found and cataloged on the Internet, there are several important "tricks" to remember. Since a search engine cannot view or understand the content of an image, you must spell it out. First, you should name the picture file with words that search engines can understand, such as "pumpkin.jpg" for a picture of a pumpkin. If you have several pumpkin pictures, name them "pumpkin_1.jpg," "pumpkin_2.jpg," etc.

Since search engines cannot view the picture but must distinguish the subject matter from the text, you should include as much explanation as possible in text form. A little knowledge of HTML is helpful. For example, the HTML image "alt" tag should include a text description of the image. The HTML "title" of the page should also contain this description.

When you include relevant words, Google Image search will be able to find your pictures, and they will be indexed and included in the search engine's database. These image searches will bring increased traffic to your Web site or blog.

to you on the computer screen may not look as good in print. It takes some experience to understand what qualities a photo must have for print media. Work with your local high school paper, for example, so that you can gain experience. Once you feel more confident, expand your jobs so that you reach out to local media outlets such as community newspapers, local PR agencies and businesses, and magazines that cover your region.

A national photography magazine called *JPG* specializes in showcasing the work of amateur or unknown photographers. Before each new issue, its editors send out requests to readers to send in up to three photos that touch upon general themes such as "street," "birthday," or "hometown." The editors choose final images, but readers can also vote for their favorites on the *JPG* Web site (jpgmag.com).

Every business that has a Web site may need photography. You might get a job photographing an employee appreciation day, the dedication of a new building, or the hiring of a new director. Even the local TV network may hire you for still images of the basketball game. If you can get a great shot and then upload it to the TV station in time for the eleven o'clock news, you might get a callback that leads to a steady freelance job. The point is that every successful opportunity can lead you to greater exposure and the potential for more (and eventually paid) work.

Keep track of all the places where your images appear. Each picture that you have published should be listed on your Web site or blog with the name of the organization where it appeared, the URL if it's still active, and the date of the photo. This should be in visual form as well as résumé form. Update your résumé every few months as your work gains exposure. Also, Internet sites may put up links without your knowledge. Every couple of months you should go into Google and check if any new Web sites are linking to your Web page or photoblog. A quick way to search for links is to use

JPG magazine (jpgmag.com) asks for photo submissions. Although editors decide which photos will be published, fellow photographers vote on their quality and how well they illustrate themes.

Google's special code. In the box where you would normally punch in search words, type link:yourwebsite. com (that is, link [colon] + yourwebsiteaddress). This will return the sites listed in Google that are linked to your site.

CHAPTER FOUR

DEFINING YOUR VISION

To grow as a photographer, examine similar work by professionals. For example, if you have experience shooting basketball games, examine the work of other sports photographers and note their techniques and what devices they use to create standout shots.

No matter what subject you prefer, you should make a scrapbook of photographers that you admire. When you find a striking image, save the Web address with a memo about what you like. If you see a good picture in a magazine, cut it out and make a hardcopy scrapbook. Examining professional pictures such as these will point you in the direction of quality image making.

Here, a zoom lens is used to photograph a football game. Try different lenses, exposure settings, shutter speeds, and apertures to get the best shots.

You may wonder how editors or art directors choose images. Although those reasons could add up, you can learn how to think more critically about your work by considering the following criteria: composition, clarity, contrast, color, pattern, texture, perspective, proportion, balance, rhythm, scale, and form.

The Internet provides easy ways to find photographs. Search engines that look for pictures, such as Google, will locate images on any topic. Other image search engines include Yahoo! (www.yahoo.com) and Picsearch (www.picsearch.com). Within time, more and better photo search engines will be developed. To find the latest, look for the phrase "image search" in a Google search. In addition, most photo-sharing sites allow searches for members and nonmembers alike.

Perhaps the most important skill in photography is composition, or the way a photo is organized visually. You should spend many hours learning effective composition and studying the work of other photographers who know how to compose well, such as Bruce Davidson, Henri Cartier-Bresson, and André Kertész. Good composition produces bold, eye-catching pictures, while poor composition results in uninteresting and unclear photos.

A series of articles about how to improve the composition of your photos can be found at www.photoinf.com.

While over time you will master the technical skills, composition requires that you develop your eye

Author Rick Doble took this photo of a county fair at night. He timed the shot so that he could capture the fireworks overhead and the carnival rides below.

for striking imagery. Since the act of taking a photograph often happens quickly, you might have to compose and shoot a photo in a matter of seconds. This practice takes a while to develop and is probably the most important skill in photography.

QUICK TIP While the best way to learn good composition is by examining the pros, you can apply basic principles, like the rule of thirds, to your images to improve your composition skills. Imagine a series of lines that divide your photo in three equal parts, horizontally and vertically. The most important areas in the picture should occur where lines intersect. Other tricks for better

What Makes a Good Photo?

A good picture has a clear subject that tells a story. Beginners often don't focus on the most important aspect, allowing things around the subject to clutter the image. For example, if the purpose of the photo is to show that a new principal is in charge of the high school, then he or she should be the center of attention and should be doing something energetic like talking to a group of students. Lighting and color should work to draw attention to the main subject.

A photo should also be sharp, with good contrast. This is essential for print reproduction. A series of pictures should tell a story when put together. The rule of thumb is that a photographer should take a long shot, a medium shot, and a close shot. All three give a good sense of the subject. For example, a long shot of a rock band might be a full shot of all the members; a medium shot might be two members playing together; and a close shot would be of the lead singer. When viewed together, these images offer a better sense of the band.

composition include shooting subjects with natural diagonals, filling the frame, and allowing more room in the direction that a subject is moving.

Although automatic exposure and focus have made photography much easier, the laws of optics still apply today as they did a century ago. Photographers should learn about exposure, aperture (f-stops), shutter speed, depth of field, and focal length. You may not realize it, but every one of these technical aspects matters whenever you take a picture. Photographers who understand how these aspects work together can create much more striking pictures than those who do not.

Since equipment is vital to photographers, you should develop a thorough knowledge of your camera. This means that you should experiment with all the various settings (in different light environments) to see the differences in picture quality. Read your manual fully and refer to it frequently. Because many photographers never read their manuals, they never utilize many of their camera's capabilities.

Digital photography relies heavily on software; therefore, it is important to learn photo-enhancing software and computer manipulation of photographs. Realize that these are two different things. With enhancing, you are bringing out and accenting what is already in the photograph. In a sense, you are using traditional darkroom techniques only in a digital manner. Computer manipulation means that you have taken the photograph one step further; by adding graphics, replacing a background in the original photo with another, or adding type on top of the image.

Eyes Wide Open

A student who wants to learn more about digital photography has many opportunities to do so. You can explore the Internet, searching for Web sites that specialize in certain subjects such as artistic and technical aspects of photography, or build a freelance business. You can also frequent popular photoblogs and personal Web pages.

This is the home page of PhotographyTips.com, a site that explains a variety of techniques for shooting just about any kind of subject, from babies to wildlife.

QUICK TIP For general photo information, as well as tips, check out the following Web sites: www.photographytips.com, www.print-digital.info, and www. takegreatpictures.com.

If your school does not offer digital photography courses, there are online courses available. Many are designed with the teen photographer in mind, are self-paced, and may be accepted for credit by your school. Their cost is often very reasonable.

If your school has a newspaper or other publication, ask to work with the current photographer. Working with someone who is more established is a great way to pick up the trade. As you improve and become more confident, you might be able take over at the school newspaper when the principal photographer graduates. Having this position on your résumé will help advance your ambitions.

CHAPTER FIVE

GETTING OUT THERE

Many successful photographers have more than one skill. They are also writers or journalists, for example. Some may have a masterful command of software such as PhotoShop that allows them to integrate photography in graphic design for desktop publishing and advertising. Still others may be accomplished Web designers. The more skills a photographer has that dovetail with photography, the greater his or her chances are at being successful.

Freelance photographers must have excellent business skills. They must be good at promotion and obtaining new jobs. They must know how to buy and maintain equipment, supplies, and software. They must

Build your portfolio by assisting a local newspaper. Learn about what photos it needs and shoot those images.

be able to keep track of income and expenses. People who are not good at business should look for a salaried position, rather than attemp to establish themselves as freelancers.

Writing is an especially important skill. Photographers are often the only reporters in a fast-changing news situation. Those who can deliver an accurate and well-written report will have a better chance of getting steady work than those who cannot. Writing is also necessary for creating accurate captions for photographs. Writing accurate background material about news photographs is essential for photojournalists.

Building a Portfolio

If the local high school does not have its newspaper online, this could be a golden opportunity for the aspiring digital photographer. Helping to put the paper online, learning how to publish on a regular basis, and understanding how to take pictures that work well with an online format could be an invaluable learning experience.

 To view images from high school and college newspapers on the Web, visit the following Web sites and directories: www. myhighschooljournalism.org, and the Yahoo! directory of school papers: dir.yahoo.com/Education/K_12/Newspapers/ Individual_School_Papers.

As was mentioned previously, some news organizations like CNN will accept photos from individuals. If your photo is selected, make sure you add it to your résumé.

MyHighSchoolJournalism.com is a showcase for online high school newspapers. Browse the site to see how photography is being used in these academic publications.

If you are accomplished and confident that you can perform, look for photo work in your hometown or city. Most local areas have a number of publications that come out on a daily, weekly, monthly, or seasonal basis. For example, there are many weekly specialty papers that reach smaller communities or more targeted audiences like senior citizens or sports fans. In addition, there may be monthly magazines for parents or health-conscious individuals. Every publication is a potential job opportunity. If you shoot the kind of images needed, you might be hired. There may also be local periodicals that are only online.

The following screenshot shows a browser window for the site ArtHelpDesk.com.

FREELANCE PHOTOGRAPHERS | ArtHelpDesk

http://www.arthelpdesk.com/

ArtHelpDesk.com   Contact Us

Freelance Photographer | Freelance Writer | Freelance Screenwriter

This is ArtHelpDesk.com, a site for freelance photographers. It locates magazines that might buy work, explains how to market your photos, and even tells you how to set up a home office.

You can find more opportunities to sell your photos by visiting www.freelance-market.net, a searchable database that's free to join.

For ideas on where to publish your photos, go to the reference section of your local library or bookstore and examine a copy of *The Photographer's Market*, which is published annually by Writer's Digest Books. Inside you'll find listings of publishers and information about what types of images they are looking for, how to properly submit your work, and general tips on selling your photos.

The Internet still has room for growth. Contrary to popular belief, most businesses are still not online and will require the services of a photographer to establish a Web presence. A photographer can find a good deal of work as these businesses create Web sites.

Investigate stock photography houses. These allow you to sell rights to your photographs. Generally, you get paid each time a photo is used. All stock houses have rules about the kind of subject matter and quality they will accept. Read these rules before you submit any images.

At the time of this writing, photo stock houses that were accepting images included Shutterstock.com, iStockPhoto.com, DreamsTime.com, BigStockPhoto.com, and CanStockPhoto.com. Before deciding to upload your images, be sure to read the image-use agreements in full. A complete directory of stock houses may be found at www.dmoz.org/Business/ Arts_and_Entertainment/Photography/Stock.

Making Connections

Building a network is an essential part of becoming successful. On your Web site or blog, provide your contact information, such as an e-mail address. You may find it useful to create a separate, free e-mail address at Yahoo.com, for example, just for your online work or business. This way, you can separate your personal e-mail from your work-related messages. You may want to include a phone number if you are looking for jobs. Also, you should participate in newsgroups that discuss

Dmoz (http://www.dmoz.org), also known as the Open Directory Project, gives a complete listing of current photography stock houses.

topics related to the information on your Web site. Send out mass e-mails to update your contacts on what you've been shooting or where your images have appeared. You could also invite people to sign up for a newsletter.

TECH TOOLS E-mail is a fast, inexpensive way to keep in touch with contacts. However, before you send out hundreds of e-mails to people, understand the rules of the Internet or you will find your e-mails blocked and your Web site banned by search engines. Never send e-mails in bulk to people who have not contacted you directly about your work. If a person has a contact address and has invited correspondence at his or her Web site, send an individual e-mail (not bulk) to that person. Do this only once. You should not send a second e-mail to this address unless the person responds to your first e-mail. If you do send bulk e-mails to people who have written to you, remind them at the top of the e-mail that they are receiving a correspondence from you because they have contacted you in the past. Remove anyone's address immediately if he or she requests it.

While e-mail works well for documents and quick notes, it is not suitable for more complex matters. Back-and-forth e-mails can take days to resolve a problem when a phone call can do it in minutes. Another situation in which the phone is better than e-mail is when you need to make a call and be online at the same time. This allows you and an editor to freely discuss a Web page while looking at it together.

Cataloging Your Photos

To work with and preserve digital photographs, you must understand picture file management. This will allow you to present, preserve, and show your work effectively. File management software that is designed just for viewing, moving, copying, renaming, and backing up picture files is essential. These software programs let you view hundreds of images rapidly so that you can easily edit your work, choosing the best images for enhancement. A rule of thumb is that you should never overwrite the original picture file that comes from your camera, and you should have one backup of all images. This means that after backing up the originals, you should rename files you want to work with so that you won't accidentally overwrite the

File management software for images is essential for locating, renaming, copying, moving, deleting, and backing up files.

original. When you do this, it is a good time to give a picture file a name that you can understand. So rather than pic12345467.jpg, which is a name that might come from your camera originally, you can rename a series of pictures from a basketball game "bball_1.jpg," "bball_2.jpg," etc.

Understanding Files and Reproduction Quality

For presenting images, learn three key concepts: file size, image size, and compression. File size refers to the size of the photo. Image size is the height and width size in pixels. Compression refers to the way a file is squeezed together so that it takes up less space on a hard drive or a Web site.

For the Internet, it is important to keep control of all three of these. Images that are too large will bleed off the screen and the browser will not be able to see the full picture. With 1024 x 768 being the standard monitor resolution, your image size should be somewhat smaller (width in pixels by height in pixels) than that for a photo to be seen altogether on the screen. A picture that is 900 X 600 should display well. (Many photo-sharing Web sites will automatically resize your images.)

File size is crucial because a large file takes a long time to download. As a result, a large photo file requires a long time before the viewer can see your image. You should try to keep your file size below 600 kilobytes.

Picture file compression is another important concept. Compression is a method by which file sizes are squeezed with a computer formula. There are two kinds of compression: lossy and lossless. The most common format, jpeg, is a lossy format that means image information gets lost as the file becomes more compressed. While such a file might be perfect for the Web or for sending as an attached file with an e-mail, you would never want to do this when storing and preserving your best images. They should be saved at full size so that there is no loss in picture quality.

However, when it comes to printing, bigger is better. Bigger uncompressed files and larger images will usually look clearer when printed. The best quality is often 300 dots per inch (dpi). This means that a 10-inch by 8-inch photo will be 3,000 pixels long by 2,400 pixels wide (10 inches X 300 dpi by 8 inches X 300 dpi). This will create a large megapixel file for higher-quality prints.

DOBLE13.JPG @ 30% (RGB/8#)

Image Size

Pixel Dimensions: 8.60M

Width: 1410 pixels

Height: 2132 pixels

OK

Cancel

Auto...

Document Size:

Width: 4.7 inches

Height: 7.107 inches

Resolution: 300 pixels/inch

☐ Scale Styles

☐ Constrain Proportions

☑ Resample Image: Bicubic

Images often need to be resized. Software allows you to increase or decrease the size of the image, depending on the need.

Learning digital photography is a worthwhile pursuit. Give yourself time to master all aspects of the craft. As you do so, you may discover that a career in photography is right for you.

GLOSSARY

aperture Also known as the f-stop, it is an adjustable opening in a lens that determines how much light hits the image plane.

blog A contraction of the term "Web log"; it is a Web journal created by an individual or a group that is arranged in chronological order.

composition The way that the elements in a photograph are organized for visual impact.

compression Computer formulas or algorithms that can reduce the size of a picture file and thus compress the file.

computer graphics Different from photography, CG involves the creation or addition of graphic elements.

depth of field More sharp focus surrounding the main subject; the smaller the aperture, the greater the depth of field.

desktop publishing Sophisticated layout for printed matter such as brochures or newsletters created with a personal computer program.

dpi "Dots per inch" is used for specifying the resolution of a digital image for printing.

file formats Pictures can be saved on a computer in different ways known as file formats; jpeg and tif are two such examples of file formats.

file size The amount of storage space on a hard drive used by a file.

focal length Determines whether a lens is set for a wide angle, a normal angle, or telephoto.

jpeg, jpg A lossy file format.

lossless compression A picture compression algorithm that does not lose any picture information.

lossy compression A picture compression algorithm that loses some picture information, but results in a much smaller file size.

pixel A single point in a digital photograph or image; photos are measured in width and height by the number of pixels on each side.

resolution The sharpness of a photograph.

shutter speed The amount of time that light is allowed to hit or expose the image plane.

tif Generally a lossless file format, although some variations are lossy.

upload/download When a file is transferred to a Web site on the Internet, this action is defined as uploading; when a file is transferred from a Web site to an individual's computer, this action is defined as downloading.

URL Uniform resource locator; the URL is the complete address of a specific page.

FOR MORE INFORMATION

American Society of Media Photographers
150 North Second Street
Philadelphia, PA 19106
(215) 451-2767
Web site: http://www.asmp.org

Aperture Foundation and Gallery
547 West 27th Street, 4th Floor
New York, NY 10001
(212) 505-5555
Web site: http://www.aperture.org

International Center of Photography (ICP)
1114 Avenue of the Americas
New York, NY 10036
(212) 857-0001
Web site: http://www.icp.edu

National Press Photographers Association
3200 Croasdaile Drive, Suite 306
Durham, NC 27705
(919) 383-7246
Web site: http://www.nppa.org

Nikon Professional Services
8120 N. Lehigh Avenue
Morton Grove, IL 60053
(800) 406-2046
Web site: http://www.authorizedphoto.com

North American Nature Photographers Association
10200 West 44th Avenue, Suite 304
Wheat Ridge, CO 80033-2840
(303) 422-8527
Web site: http://www.nanpa.org

Professional Photographers of America
229 Peachtree Street NE, Suite 2200
Atlanta, GA 30303
(404) 522-8600
Web site: http://www.ppa.com

Web Sites

Due to the changing nature of Internet links, Rosen
Publishing has developed an online list of Web sites
related to the subject of this book. This site is updated
regularly. Please use this link to access the list:

http://www.rosenlinks.com/dcb/cbdp

FOR FURTHER READING

Borowsky, Irvin J. *Opportunities in Photography Careers*. New York, NY: McGraw-Hill, 2004.

Burian, Peter, and Bob Caputo. *National Geographic Photography Field Guide: Secrets to Making Great Pictures*, 2nd ed. Hanover, PA: National Geographic, 2003.

Campbell, Marc, and Dave Long. *Digital Photography for Teens*. Boston, MA: Thomson Course Technology PTR, 2006.

Eismann, Katrin, Sean Duggan, and Tim Grey. *Real World Digital Photography*. Berkeley, CA: Peachpit Press, 2003.

Frost, Lee. *Teach Yourself Photography*. New York, NY: McGraw-Hill, 2004.

Hurn, David. *On Being a Photographer: A Practical Guide*. Anacortes, WA: Lenswork Publishing, 2004.

Jenkins, Henry. "Confronting the Challenges of Participatory Culture: Media Education for the 21st Century." The John D. and Catherine T. MacArthur Foundation. 2006. Retrieved January 24, 2007 (http://www.macfound.org/site/c.lkLXJ8MQKrH/b.1038727/apps/s/content.asp?ct=2946895).

King, Julie Adair. *Shoot Like a Pro! Digital Photography Techniques*. New York, NY: McGraw-Hill Osborne Media, 2003.

London, Barbara, and Jim Stone. *A Short Course in Photography: An Introduction to Photographic Technique*, 6th ed. New York, NY: Prentice Hall Press, 2005.

Long, Ben. *Complete Digital Photography*, 3rd ed. Clifton
    Park, NY: Delmar Thompson Learning, 2004.

McLean, Cheryl. *Careers for Shutterbugs and Other Candid
    Types*. New York, NY: McGraw-Hill, 2002.

Paterson, Freeman. *Photography and the Art of Seeing: A
    Visual Perception Workshop for Film and Digital
    Photography*. Toronto, ON: Key Porter Books, 2004.

Rice, Patrick. *Digital Portrait Photography of Teens and
    Seniors: Shooting and Selling Techniques for
    Photographers*. Buffalo, NY: Amherst Media, 2005.

BIBLIOGRAPHY

Bureau of Labor Statistics, U.S. Department of Labor. "Photography Careers, Jobs, and Employment Information." 2004. Retrieved October 30, 2006 (http://www.careeroverview.com/photography-careers.html).

Dorfman, John. *Columbia Journalism Review*, "The New Forces That Threaten Photojournalism." 2005. Retrieved November 9, 2006 (http://www.cjr.org/issues/2002/4/photo-dorfman.asp).

Harris Interactive. "National Survey of College Students Provides '10 Best Tips' to Marketers." 2003. Retrieved November 8, 2006 (http://www.harrisinteractive.com/news/allnewsbydate.asp?NewsID=575).

Photography.com. "Film vs. Digital Statistics." 2006. Retrieved November 16, 2006 (http://www.photography.com/film-vs-digital-statistics.php).

Romano, Amy. *Cool Careers Without College for People Who Love Everything Digital*. New York, NY: Rosen Publishing Group, Inc., 2007.

Roza, Greg. *Careers as a Professional Photographer*. New York, NY: Rosen Publishing Group, Inc., 2001.

Wikipedia. "Digital Photography." Retrieved November 3, 2006 (http://en.wikipedia.org/wiki/Digital_photography).

INDEX

About the Author

Since photographer and author Rick Doble created his personal photography Web site in 1998 (www.RickDoble. net), it has been viewed by more than half a million people. Doble's work has been reviewed by a major photography magazine in the United States and by critics worldwide. Students in high school, college, and graduate school have studied his images and used them for papers and projects, and he has been invited to display his work with a number of Web sites, symposiums, and museums. His work has also appeared on the covers of CDs, books, and e-zines.

Photo Credits

Cover, p. 1 © www.istockphoto.com; p. 4 © www. shutterstock.com/Patricia Malina; pp. 6, 16, 21, 23, 39, 53 © Rick Doble; p. 20 © www.shutterstock.com/Dimitrije Paunovic; p. 37 © www.shutterstock.com/Susana Guimarães de Carvalho; p. 44 © www.shutterstock.com/ Marco Regalia.

Designer: Nelson Sá
Photo Researcher: Amy Feinberg